100% Funny
Mexican Jokes

The Best, Funniest, Dirty, Short and Long Mexican Jokes Book

R. Cristi

Author Online!
For updates and more jokes
visit R. Cristi page at

www.bestjokebooks.com

100% Funny Mexican Jokes:
The Best, Funniest, Dirty, Short and Long Mexican
Jokes Book
by R. Cristi

ISBN 978-0-9866004-0-1

Printed in the United States of America

Copyright © 2010 Psylon Press

Other Books in the Series

100% Blonde Jokes
ISBN 978-0-9866004-1-8

100% SMS Jokes
(Forthcoming)

100% Short Jokes
(Forthcoming)

The Mexican Border

Jose arrives at the Mexican border on his bike with 2 huge bags over his shoulders. The guard stops him and asks: "What's in the bags?"

"Senior, It's only sand." replies Jose.

"Sand? Well, we'll just see about that - get off the bike!"

The guard takes the bags, rips them open, empties them out and finds nothing in them... except sand. Detaining Jose overnight, the sand is analyzed, but only to discover it is in fact simply sand.

Jose is released, the sand is put into new bags and placed on Jose's shoulders, and he is let across the border.

Next day, same thing happens. The guard asks: "What you got there?"

"Sand," says Jose.

A thorough examination of the bags again shows there to be nothing but sand, and subsequently Jose is allowed to ride across the border.

For a whole year this continues until one day Jose doesn't show up, and the guard discovers him in a Cantina in Mexico.

"Hey, Bud," says the guard, "I know you're smuggling something. For a year it's driven me crazy. It's all I can think about... I can't get sleep, the kids are getting neglected... heck, even the dog senses I'm beginning to lose it! Between you and me, just what are you smuggling?"

Jose sips his beer, smiles and replies: "Bicycles..."

I Only Need $10

Jose and Carlos are panhandlers...

They panhandle on different areas of town. Carlos panhandles just as long as Jose but only collects 2 to 3 dollars every day.

Jose brings home a suitcase FULL of $10 bills, drives a Mercedes, lives in a mortgage free house and has a lot of money to spend.

Carlos says to Jose "I work just as long and hard as you do but how do you bring home a suitcase full of $10 bills every day?"

Jose says, "Look at your sign, what does it say?"

Carlos sign reads: 'I have no work, a wife and 6 kids to support.'

Jose says "No wonder you only get $2-3 dollars."

Carlos says "So what does your sign say?"

Jose shows Carlos his sign... It reads : 'I only need another $10 to move back to Mexico.

Two American Pigs and a Mexican

Two American pigs and a Mexican will be sent to the moon. The ground controller does the final check up.

"Pig# 1, do you read?"

"Groink, yes, this is pig #1."

"Do you know what to do?"

"Groink. Yes, when we leave earth, I push the green button and navigate the spaceship to the moon."

"Good, now pig # 2 do you know what to do ?

"Groink. When we return to earth, I push the white button and navigate back."

"Very good. Mexican, do you know what to do."

"Yes, don't touch anything and feed the pigs..."

Traveling Through Amazon Region

There were 3 men traveling through Amazon region, a Mexican, a German and an American and Amazon people have catch them.

The chief of their tribe have said to German, "What would you want to have on your back during whipping? Germ have said, "I wanna oil!" This is why they put oil on his back, right after a large Amazons whips him 10 times. After he had finished the German have had huge welts on the back, and he was so week so he could hardly move.

Chef haul the German away, soon after he said to Mexican Man, "What will be on your back?" "I am taking nothing!" , and he takes his ten lashings without a single flinch. At last Amazons have asked American the same question.

He responds, "I'll take the Mexican."

Bungee-jumping in Mexico

Two guys are bungee-jumping one day. The first guy says to the second. "You know, we could make a lot of money running our own bungee-jumping service in Mexico." The second guy thinks this is a great idea, so the two pool their money and buy everything they'll need - a tower, an elastic cord, insurance, etc.

They travel to Mexico and begin to set up on the square. As they are constructing the tower, a crowd begins to assemble. Slowly, more and more people gather to watch them at work. The first guy jumps. He bounces at the end of the cord, but when he comes back up, the second guy notices that he has a few cuts and scratches.

Unfortunately, the second guy isn't able catch him, he falls again, bounces and comes back up again. This time, he is bruised and bleeding. Again, the second guy misses him.

The first guy falls again and bounces back up. This time, he comes back pretty messed up - he's got a couple of broken bones and is almost unconscious. Luckily, the second guy finally catches him this time and says, "What happened? Was the cord too long?"

The first guy says, "No, the cord was fine, but what the heck is a 'pinata'?"

All In A Boat

There is an American, a German, and a Mexican. They are all in a boat.

The boat is about to sink. Each of them have to throw things out to make the boat lighter!

The German throws out 4 cases of beer and says: "We have a lot of bear in Germany so we don't need these!"

The Mexican throws out 5 cases of burritos and says: "We have a lot of burritos in Mexico so we don't need these!"

The American grabs the Mexican and throws him out. The German asks why he threw the Mexican out. And the American replies: "We have a lot of Mexicans in America so we don't need him!

A Big Earthquake

A big earthquake with the strength of 8.1 on the Richter scale hits Mexico. Two million Mexicans have died and over a million are injured. The country is totally ruined and the government doesn't know where to start with asking for help to rebuild. The rest of the world is in shock.

Canada is sending troopers to help the Mexican army control the riots.

Saudi Arabia is sending oil to replace what was lost.

Other Latin American countries are sending supplies to replace what was lost.

The European community is sending food to replace what was lost.

The United States, not to be outdone, is sending two million replacement Mexicans.

Mexican Boy

A small Mexican boy went into the kitchen where his mom was baking. He puts his hand in the flour and wipes it all over his face. He says: "Mamita, look at me - I'm a white boy!"

His mom slaps him in the face and says:

"Dios mio, you must be joking, go show that to your father!"

He goes to his dad who was in the living room and says: "Look, I'm a white boy."

His dad slaps him hard in the face and says: "Go show that to your grandma."

The boy goes into his grandma's room and says: "Mira, Abuelita, yo soy a white boy."

His grandmother slaps him in the face and sends him back to his mother.

His mother says: "See, did you learn anything from that?"

To which the boy replies:

"Sure did! I have only been white for five minutes and I already hate you Mexicans!"

Mexican Buying Socks

A Mexican, who speaks no English, comes to the USA. As is often the case, he finds that he needs new socks. So, he walks into a clothing store, and manages to convey to the clerk that he needs something, but not what.

So, the clerk starts taking down boxes and showing what's inside to the Mexican. He shows him a shirt, some pants, a tie, a hat, but each time the Mexican shakes his head and says "No."

Finally, the clerk brings down a box of socks and shows them to the Mexican. The Mexican starts nodding vigorously and says "¡Eso sí que es!"

The clerk angrily blurts out, "Well why didn't you just spell it in the first place?!"

Mexican Maid

Aimara, a Mexican maid announced to her Boss Mr Blanco and his wife that she was quitting. When asked why, she replied, "I'm in the family way."

The wife was totally surprised and shocked, and asked who it was.

The maid replied, "Your husband and your son."

Mrs Blanco was mortified and demanded an explanation.

"Well," Aimara explained, "I go to the library to clean it and your husband say, 'You are in the way'. I go to the living room to clean and your son say 'You are in my way'. So I'm in the family way and I quit."

We Are In Mexico

A German, an Australian, and a Mexican are on a plane. They say that they can tell where they are by sticking their hands out of the pane.

The German sticks his hand out and says "We are in Germany". The others ask, "How do you know", the German says, "Because it's so cold".

Then the Australian sticks his hand out and says "We are in Australia", the others ask "How do you know", he replies "Because it's so warm".

Then the Mexican sticks his hand out and back in. He says " We are in Mexico", the others ask "How do you know", he says " Because my watch is gone"

Mexican/American War

During the Mexican/American war, an intense long standoff occurred along the front. For days and days neither side made any advances. Finally, an American general had a bright idea.

He aimed his rifle to the Mexican trenches and yelled "Hey Juan!"... A soldier jumped up and replied "What?" The general shot him dead. This continued for three days.

A Mexican general decided that he too could play this game and decided to try it out. He called out "Hey John!" An American replied "John isn't here... is that you Juan?"

The Mexican general stood up, "Yeah?!"

Eating Lunch

An Irishman, a Mexican and a redneck were doing construction work on the scaffolding of a tall building. They were eating lunch. The Irishman said, "Corned beef and cabbage! If I get corned beef and cabbage one more time for lunch, I'm going to jump off this building."

The Mexican opened his lunch box and exclaimed, "Burritos again! If I get burritos one more time, I'm going to jump off too." The redneck opened his lunch and said, "Bologna again. If I get a bologna sandwich one more time, I'm jumping too."

Next day the Irishman opens his lunch box, sees corned beef and cabbage and jumps to his death. The Mexican opens his lunch, sees a burrito and jumps too. The redneck opens his lunch, sees the bologna and jumps to his death as well.

At the funeral, the Irishman's wife is weeping. She says, "If I'd known how really tired he was of corned beef and cabbage, I never would have given it to him again!"

The Mexican's wife also weeps and says, "I could have given him tacos or enchiladas! I didn't realize he hated burritos so much."

Everyone turned and stared at the redneck's wife. "Hey, don't look at me," she said. "He makes his own lunch."

Mexican Bandit

A Mexican bandit made a specialty of crossing the Rio Grande from time to time and robbing banks in Texas. Finally, a reward was offered for his capture, and an enterprising Texas ranger decided to track him down.

After a lengthy search, he traced the bandit to his favorite cantina, snuck up behind him, put his trusty six-shooter to the bandit's head, and said, "You're under arrest. Tell me where you hide the loot or I'll blow your brains out."

But the bandit didn't speak English, and the Ranger didn't speak Spanish. Fortunately, a bilingual lawyer was in the saloon and translated the Ranger's message. The terrified bandit blurted out, in Spanish, that the loot was buried under the oak tree in back of the cantina.

"What did he say?" asked the Ranger.

The lawyer answered, "He said 'Get lost, you turkey. You wouldn't dare shoot me."

God Messed with Human's Brains

God wonders what would happen if he took the left side of the man's brain out. He does it and the man now counts: 2, 4, 6, etc...

So God thinks, ok, cool. What would happen if I put the left side back in and took out the right side? So he does it, and the man starts counting: 1, 3, 5, etc...

God thinks, ok, let's see what happens if I take both sides of his brain out? He does it and the man starts counting: uno, dos, tres...

Mexican Fisherman

The American investment banker was at the pier of a small coastal Mexican village when a small boat with just one fisherman docked. Inside the small boat were several large yellow fin tuna. The American complimented the Mexican on the quality of his fish and asked how long it took to catch them.

The Mexican replied, "Only a little while."

The American then asked, "Why didn't you stay out longer and catch more fish?"

The Mexican said, "With this I have more than enough to support my family's needs."

The American then asked, "But what do you do with the rest of your time?"

The Mexican fisherman said, "I sleep late, fish a little, play with my children, take siesta with my wife, Maria, stroll into the village each evening where I sip wine and play guitar with my amigos, I have a full and busy life."

The American scoffed, "I am a Harvard MBA and could help you. You should spend more time fishing; and with the proceeds, buy a bigger boat: With the proceeds from the bigger boat you could buy several boats. Eventually you would have a fleet of fishing boats. Instead of selling your catch to a middleman you would sell directly to the processor; eventually opening your own cannery. You would control the product, processing and distribution. You would need to leave this small coastal fishing village and move to Mexico City, then Los Angeles and eventually New York where you will run your ever-expanding enterprise."

The Mexican fisherman asked, "But, how long will this all take?"

To which the American replied, "15 to 20 years."

"But what then?" asked the Mexican.

The American laughed and said that's the best part. "When the time is right you would announce an IPO and sell your company stock to the public and become very rich, you would make millions."

"Millions?... Then what?"

The American said, "Then you would retire. Move to a small coastal fishing village where you would sleep late, fish a little, play with your kids, take siesta with your wife, stroll to the village in the evenings where you could sip wine and play your guitar with your amigos."

Flying Across Country

An Englishman, Frenchman, Mexican, and Texan were flying across country on a small plane when the pilot comes on the loud speaker and says "We're having mechanical problems and the only way we can make it to the next airport is for 3 of you to open the door and jump, at least one of you can survive"

The four open the door and look out below. The Englishman takes a deep breath and hollers "God Save The Queen" and jumps.

The Frenchman gets really inspired and hollers "Vive La France" and he also jumps.

This really pumps up the Texan so he hollers "Remember the Alamo" and he grabs the Mexican and throws him out of the plane.

Parachute Jumping

There were three men, a Mexican, Serbian, and a Russian, on a plane along with a fat woman and 3 parachutes. The plane started going down, and the 3 men grabbed the parachutes.

The Mexican jumped out yelling, "God bless Mexico!"

The Serbian jumped out and screamed, "God bless Serbia!"

The Russian jumped out yelling, "God bless mother Russia!"

The fat woman jumped out without a parachute and yelled, "God bless whoever I land on!"

Mexican Jews

Sid and Mundo were sitting in a Mexican restaurant. "Sid," asked Mundo, "Are there any Jews in Mexico?"

I don't know," Mundo replied. "Why don't we ask the waiter?"

When the waiter came by, Mundo asked him, "Are there any Mexican Jews?"

"I don't know Sir, let me ask," the waiter replied, and he went into the kitchen. He returned in a few minutes and said, "No, Sir. No Mexican Jews."

"Are you sure?" Mundo asked.

"I will check again, Sir." the waiter replied and went back to the kitchen.

While he was still gone, Sid said, "I cannot believe there are no Jews in Mexico. Our people are scattered everywhere."

When the waiter returned he said, "Sir, no Mexican Jews."

"Are you really sure?" Mundo asked again. "I cannot believe there are no Mexican Jews."

"Sir, I ask everyone," the waiter replied exasperated. "We have orange Jews, prune Jews, tomato Jews, and grape Jews, but no one ever hear of Mexican Jews!"

Pacific Coast Highway

Two Mexicans are riding along Pacific Coast Highway on a motorcycle. They break down and start hitching a lift.

A friendly trucker stops to see if he can help and the Mexicans ask him for a lift. He tells them he has no room in the truck as he is carrying 20,000 bowling balls.

The Mexicans put it to the driver that if they can manage to fit in the back with their bike will he take them and he agrees.

They manage to squeeze themselves and their motorbike into the back of the truck so the driver shuts the doors and gets off on his way.

By this time he is really late and so puts his foot down.

Sure enough the Highway Patrol pulls him over for speeding. The good officer asks the driver what he is carrying to which he replies jokingly-- "Mexican eggs".

The policeman obviously doesn't believe this so wants to take a look. He opens the back door and quickly shuts it and locks it. He gets on his radio and calls for immediate backup from as many officers as possible. The dispatcher asks what emergency he has that requires so many officers.

"I've got a truck with 20,000 Mexican eggs in it - 2 have hatched and the bastards have managed to steal a motorcycle already.

Watch the Olympics

Three guys, one Chinese, one French, and one Mexican wanted to watch the Olympics but didn't have any money to buy tickets. The Chinese guy suddenly gets an idea and went home to fetch his bicycle.

He rode up to the security guard at the gate and yells, "China, bicycling.! Hurry, let me in, I'm late!" The guard, not wanting to jeopardize his job, lets the Chinese guy through.

Seeing that this idea worked, the French guy runs home and grabs a long pole and runs back to the security guard and yells, "France, pole vaulting! Let me in, I'm late!" The security guard lets the French guy through.

Seeing how great their ideas were, the Mexican runs home and grabs a chain link fence, wraps the fence around his body and hops up to the security guard and yells, "Mexico, fencing!"

You Know You Are a Mexican When...

- You share the same social security number with all your amigos.

- You smell like BO all the time.

- You don't know what BO is.

- You have at least thirty cousins.

- There is at least one member in your family named Maria, Guadalupe, Juan, Jose, or Jesus.

- You run and hide when you see the Border Patrol.

- You see a fence and want to hop over it.

- You are too short to go on rides at Disneyland.

- You mow lawns for a living.

- You fart more than you breathe.

- Your mother yells at the top of her lungs to call you to dinner even if it's a one bedroom apartment.

- You are in a five-passenger car with eight people in it.

No Mexicans Please

A U.S. Navy cruiser pulled into port in Mississippi for a week's liberty. The first evening, the Captain was more than a little surprised to receive the following letter from the wife of a wealthy plantation owner:

"Dear Captain, Thursday will be my daughter Melinda's, coming of age party. I would like you to send four well mannered, handsome, unmarried officers. They should arrive at 8 p.m. prepared for an evening of polite southern conversation and dance with lovely young ladies. One last point: No, Mexicans. We don't like Mexicans."

Sure enough, at 8 p.m. on Thursday, the lady heard a rap at the door. She opened the door to find, in dress uniform, four exquisitely mannered, smiling black officers. Her jaw hit the floor, but pulling herself together she stammered, "There must be some mistake!"

"On no, madam," said the first officer, "Captain Martinez doesn't make mistakes."

Big Tough Mexican Guy

A big tough Mexican man married a good-looking Mexican lady and after the wedding, laid down the following rules:

"Honey, I'll be home when I want, if I want and at what time I want – and I don't expect any hassle from you. I expect a great dinner to be on the table unless I tell you otherwise. I'll go hunting, fishing, boozing, and card-playing when I want with my old buddies and don't you give me a hard time about it.

Those are my rules! Any comments?"

His lovely new bride said, "No, that's fine with me. Just understand that there'll be sex here at eight o'clock every night – whether you're here or not."

Short Questions & Answers

Q. Why do Mexicans have small stearing wheels?
A. So they can drive with handcuffs on.

Q. Why don't Mexicans play hide and seek?
A. Cause nobody will look for them.

Q. What's a Mexican favorite book store?
A. Borders.

Q. A bunch of Mexicans are running down a hill, what is going on?
A. A prison break.

Q. Did you hear about that one Mexican that went to college?
A. Yeah.. me neither.

Q. Did you hear about the winner of the Mexican beauty contest?
A. Me neither.

Q. How do you get 50 Mexicans is a phone booth?
A. Throw food stamps in it.

Q. How do you starve a Mexican?
A. Put their food stamps in their work boots.

Q. How do you stop a Mexican from robbing your house?
A. Put up a help-wanted sign.

Q. How do you stop a Mexican tank?
A. Shoot the guy pushing it.

Q. How many Mexicans does it take to screw in a light bulb?
A. Doesn't matter, they're to short to reach the socket.

Q. Juan, Carlos and Antonio all jump off a cliff to see who will hit the ground first. Who wins?
A. Society.

Q. What are the first 3 words in every Mexican cookbook?
A. Steal a chicken.

Q. What do Mexicans pick in the off season?
A. Their nose.

Q. What do you call 100 Mexicans working on a roof?
A. Chingos.

Q. What do you call 4 Mexicans in quicksand?
A. Cuatro Cinco.

Q. What do you call a Mexican driving a BMW?
A. Grand Theft Auto.

Q. What do you call a Mexican with a rubber toe?
A. Roberto.

Q. What do you call a Mexican without a lawn mower?
A. Unemployed.

Q. What do you do when a Mexican is riding a bike?
A. Chase after him, it's probably yours!

Q. What is it when a Mexican is taking a shower?
A. A miracle.

Q. What is the greatest Mexican invention?
A. A solar powered flash light.

Q: What do you call a building full of Mexicans?
A: Jail.

Q. What's the difference between a bench and a Mexican?
A. A bench can support a family.

Q. Why are Mexicans so short?
A. They all live in basement apartments.

Q. Why are Mexicans so short?
A. When they're young, their parents say, "When you get bigger you have to get a good job."

Q. Why do Mexicans drive low riders?
A. They are too short to get into any other type of car.

Q. Why do Mexicans re-fry their beans?
A. Have you seen a Mexican do anything right the first time?

Q. Why wasn't Jesus born in Mexico?
A. He couldn't find 3 wise men or a virgin.

Q. Why don't Mexicans BBQ?
A. The beans fall through the little holes.

Q. Why does a Mexican eat Tomales for Christmas?
A. So they have something to unwrap.

Q. What are the first 3 words in the Mexican national anthem?
A. Attention K-Mart shoppers.

Q. Why doesn't Mexico have a Olympic team?
A. Because every Mexican that can run, jump, and swim is already across the border!

Q. How many officers does it take to arrest a Mexican guy?
A. It takes 4; 1 to arrest him and 3 to carry his oranges.

Q: What do you get when you cross a Mexican and an Iranian?
A: Oil of Ol'e.

Q: Why did the Mexicans fight so hard to take the Alamo?
A: So they could have four clean walls to write on.

Q: Why do Mexicans eat beans every day?
A: So they can take a bubble bath at night.

Q: What's the difference between a Jewish girl and a Mexican girl?
A: The Mexican girl has real orgasms and fake jewelry!

Q: What do you call two Mexicans playing basketball?
A: Juan on Juan.

Q: Do you know what Mexican will get as birthday present.
A: Your bike !

Q: How do you find out the population of Mexico?
A: Drop a peso on the ground.

Q: Who's the richest person in Mexico?
A: The person who finds the quarter!

Q: What's the difference between a white and a Mexican?
A: A shower.

Q: What do you call a Taco with a food stamp inside it?
A: A Mexican fortune cookie.

Q: What do you call 3 Mexicans in quick sand?
A: Bean Dip.

Q: Why do Mexicans cross the border in any number except 3?
A: Because the signs say no trespassing.

Spicy Dinners

Q: How do you start a Mexican parade?
A: You throw a penny in the road.

Q: How come there aren't any Mexicans on Star Trek?
A: They don't work in the future, either.

Q: What do you get when you cross a Mexican and a German?
A: A Beaner-Schnitzel.

Q: What do you call a Mexican quarterback?
A: El Paso.

Q: Why doesn't Mexico have a NAVY?
A: Because cardboard don't float.

Q: What do you call a Mexican in a two-story house?
A: Adopted.

Q: What do you call a Mexican guy who lost his car?
A: Carlos....

Q: Why a Mexican can't be one of the 11/11 terrorists?
A: They are always late, and would have missed all 4 flights.

Q: Why did the Mexican rush to the discount store?
A: The ad said: "Beans for sale!"

Q: Why did Coke fire the Mexican?
A: He kept trying to SNIFF it instead of DRINK it.

Q: What is the difference between a Mexican and an elevator?
A: One can raise a child.

Q: Did you hear about the two car pile-up in the Wal-Mart parking lot?
A: 50 Mexicans died.

Q: Why do Mexican kids walk around school like they own the place?
A: Because their dads built it and their mom clean it.

Q: What's a Mexican's favorite sport?
A: Cross country.

Q: Why can't Mexicans play uno?
A: Because they always steal the green card.

Q: 2 Mexicans are in a car, who is driving?
A: A cop.

Q: What do you call a group of stoned Mexicans?
A: Baked beans.

Q: When a Mexican runs into a wall whats the first thing that hits?
A: His lawn mower.

Q: A black guy and a Mexican jump off a building, who dies first?
A: Who cares?

Q: What is Mexican overdrive?
A: Putting the car in neutral and rolling down a hill.

Q: Whats the definition of a Mexican Slut?
A: Frito Lay.

Q: What do you call a hardworking Mexican?
A: Low Pay.

Q: There is a bus full of Mexicans, who's driving?
A: Boarder Patrol.

Q: What do you call a Mexican picking cotton?
A: A niggers job.

Q: What do you call your boss if he is Mexican?
A: Impossible.

Q: Why can't Mexicans become doctors?
A: It's too hard to spray paint prescriptions.

Q: How do 3 Mexicans cross the Rio Grande?
A: One swims and the other two walked on the dead fish.

Q: Why don't Mexicans marry blacks?
A: Their kids would be too lazy to steal.

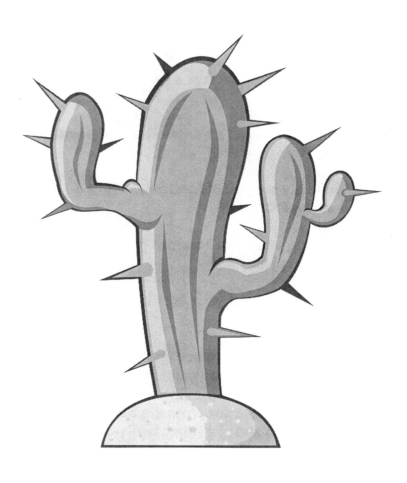

Q: Why did the Mexican government cancel both drivers education and sex education in school?
A: The donkey died.

Q: What do you say to a Mexican in a three-piece suit?
A: Will the defendant please rise!

Q: What do you call a Mexican with a dog?
A: A vegetarian !

Q: Why don't Mexicans have checking accounts?
A: It's too hard to spray paint your name on the little line.

Q: What do you call a Mexican with a vasectomy?
A: A Dry Martinez.

Q: What is the name of Mexico's telephone company?
A: "Taco Bell."

Q: What would you call a Mexican gigolo?
A: Juan For The Money!

Q: Why is there so little great Mexican literature?
A: Spray paint wasn't invented until 1950.

Q: Why is the average age of the Mexican army, 40?
A: Because they take 'em right out of high school!

Q: Why do Mexicans pick at their belly buttons when their plates are clean?
A: They want an after-dinner lint.

Q: Why are there no Mexican pharmacies?
A: They can't figure out how to put the little bottles in the typewriter.

Q: What happened to the Mexicans National Library?
A: Someone stole the book.

Q: What do you get when you cross a Mexican and a squirrel?
A: A tree full of hubcaps.

Q: What do you call a Mexican at a university?
A: The caretaker.

Q: What did the Mexican do with his first fifty cent piece?
A: He married her.

Q: What are the three most difficult years in a Mexican's life?
A: Second grade.

Q: How many Mexicans does it take to eat an armadillo?
A: Three, one to eat it and two to watch for cars.

Q: How many Mexican men does it take to do the washing up?
A: None it's woman's work!

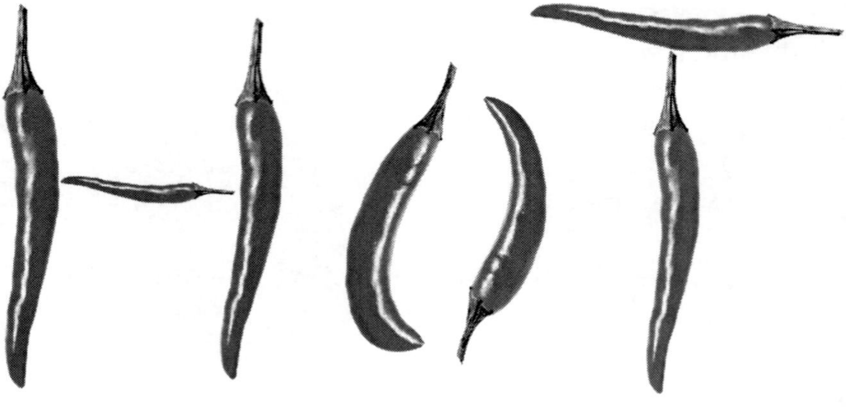

Q: How does the Mexican prepare for a trip in Alaska?
A: He packs a six-pack in case he has to leave a message in the snow.

Q: How does a Mexican count?
A: "1, 2, 3, another, another, another...."

Q: How do you break a Mexican's finger?
A: Punch him in the nose.

Q: How can you tell a Mexican woman is on her period?
A: She's only wearing one sock.

Q: Have you heard about the Mexican 500 car race?
A: The first car to start wins.

Q: Did you hear about the Mexican terrorist sent to blow up a car?
A: He burned his mouth on the tailpipe.

Q: Did you hear about the Mexican lesbian?
A: She loved men.

Q: What is the best selling deodorant in Mexico?
A: Raid.

Q: What do you call a kid that's half Mexican and half Polish?
A: Retardo.

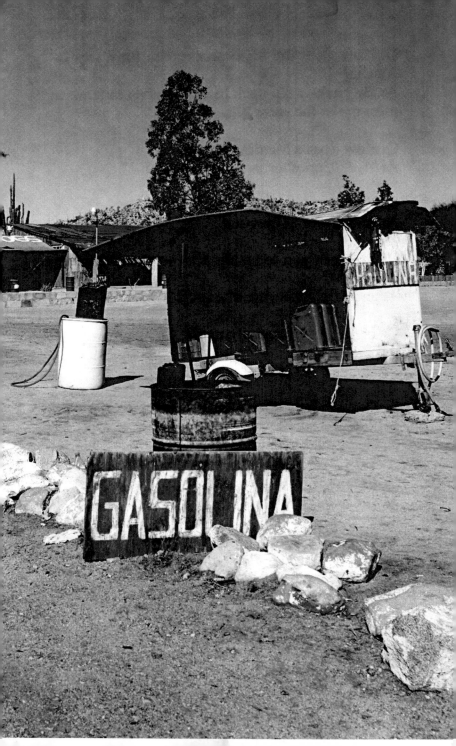

Q: How many Mexican mechanics does it take to lube a car?
A: One if you back over him twice.

Q: What do you call a Mexican queer?
A: A senor eater.

Q: What do you call a little Mexican?
A: A paragraph, because he's not quite an essay.

Q: Why don't you throw a rock at a Mexican on a bike?
A: Because it's probably your bike.

Q: What do a Mexican and a sperm have in common?
A: Only one out of a million work.

Q: Why did the Mexican cross the road?
A: To get from abco to the orange groves.

Q: Why did the Mexicans have to move out of the house?
A: Because they couldn't figure out how to flush the pool.

Q: What do a Mexican and a skunk have in common?
A: They are both black and white and they both smell.

Q: What do you get when you cross a Mexican and a dumb blonde?
A: A kid who spray paints his name on a chain link fence.

Q: Why don't Mexicans play hide and seek?
A: Because no one will look for them.

Q: Why do Mexicans make great astronauts?
A: Because they take up space in school.

Q: What do you call a Mexican with a fur coat?
A: A pipe cleaner.

Q: How does every Mexican joke start?
A: The teller looks over both his shoulders.

Q: How do you save a Mexican from drowning?
A: Take your foot off his head.

Q: What is the best boxing a Mexican does?
A: Oranges.

Q: How do you get a Mexican out of a bath tub?
A: Throw in a bar of soap.

Q: What do a Mexican and an Oreo have in common?
A: They are both black and white and come in packs of 40.

Q: What do you call a Mexican sky diver?
A: Instant air pollution.

Appendix

Bonus

Blonde Jokes

The following jokes are from my book
100% Blonde Jokes.

Give Her Another Chance

One day a big group of blondes met in New York to show the world that blondes aren't dumb.
They begged: "Ask any of us any question, and we will show you that we're not dumb."

The group caught the attention of a passer by, who volunteered to ask them some questions. He climbed up on a car and randomly picked a blonde out of the crowd.

She got up on the car too and the man asked: "What is the first month of the year?"
The blonde responded: "November?"

"Nope," said the man. At this point the crowd began to chant, "Give her another chance, give her another chance."

So the man asked: "What is the capital of the USA ?"
The blonde responded: "Paris?"
So the crowd began chanting again: "Give her another chance, give her another chance."

The man said: "Okay, but this is the last one. What is one plus one?"
The blonde replied: "Two?"
"Give her another chance, Give her another chance." screamed the crowd.

Passed Away

Sally goes to work one morning crying her eyes out. Her boss, concerned his employee, walks over to her and asks sympathetically, "What's the matter?" The blonde replies, "Early this morning I got a phone call that my mother had passed away."

The boss, feeling very sorry at this point suggests to the young girl, "Why don't you go home for the day... we aren't terribly busy. Just take the day off and go relax."

Sally very calmly states, "No I'd be better off here. I need to keep my mind busy and I have the best chance of doing that here."

The boss agrees and allows her to work as usual. "If you need anything just let me know" says the boss.

A few hours pass and the boss decides to check on Sally. He looks out his office and sees her crying hysterically.

He rushes over an asks, "What's the matter now? Are you going to be OK?"

Sally breaks down in tears. "I just received a horrible call from my sister. She said that her mom died too!"

At the Bus Stop

Two blonds are waiting at a bus stop.

When a bus pulls up and opens the door, one of the blonds leans inside and asks the bus driver: "Will this bus take me to 5th Avenue?"

The bus driver shakes his head and says, "No, I'm sorry."

Hearing this, the other blond leans inside, smiles, and twitters:

"Will it take ME?"

Oklahoma Blondes

Two blondes living in Oklahoma were sitting on a bench talking ... and one blonde says to the other, "Which do you think is farther away ... Florida or the moon?"

The other blonde turns and says "Helloooooooooo, can you see Florida ...?"

Blonde Guy

A blonde guy gets home early from work and hears strange noises coming from the bedroom. He rushes upstairs to find his wife naked on the bed, sweating and panting. "What's up?" he says. "I'm having a heart attack," cries the woman.

He rushes downstairs to grab the phone, but just as he's dialing, his 4-year-old son comes up and says, "Daddy! Daddy! Uncle Ted's hiding in your closet and he's got no clothes on!"

The guy slams the phone down and storms upstairs into the bedroom, past his screaming wife, and rips open the wardrobe door.

Sure enough, there is his brother, totally naked, cowering on the closet floor.

You rotten bastard, "says the husband, "my wife's having a heart attack and you're running around naked scaring the kids!

One Minute

A British Airways employee took a call from a blonde asking the question, "How long is the Concorde flight from London to New York?"

"Um, just a minute, if you please," he murmured.

Then, as he turned to check the exact flight time, he heard an equally polite, "Thank you," as the phone went dead.

Lesbian

A blonde guy was sitting in a bar when he spots a very pretty young woman. He advances towards her when the bartender says to him, "Don't waste your time on that one. She's a lesbian."

The blonde goes over to her anyway and says, "So which part of Lesbia are you from?"

Polish Priest

A blonde was telling a priest a Polish joke, when halfway through the priest interrupts her, "Don't you know I'm Polish?"

"Oh, I'm sorry," the blonde apologizes, "Do you want me to start over and talk slower?"

The Bet

A blonde and a redhead met for dinner after work and were watching the 6 o'clock news. A man was shown threatening to jump from the Brooklyn Bridge. The blonde bet the redhead $50 that he wouldn't jump, and the redhead replied, "I'll take that bet!"

Anyway, sure enough, he jumped, so the blonde gave the redhead the $50 she owned. The redhead said, "I can't take this, you're my friend." The blonde said, "No. A bet's a bet."

So the redhead said, "Listen, I have to admit, I saw this one on the 5 o'clock news, so I can't take your money."

The blonde replied, "Well, so did I, but I never thought he'd jump again!"

Dumb Blonde Crooks

Two blonde robbers were robbing a hotel. The first one said, "I hear sirens. Jump!"

The second one said, "But we're on the 13th floor!"

The first one screamed back, "This is no time to be superstitious."